More Than A Job

Making Lifestyle Choices
With God at the Centre

Jani Rubery

LIFESTYLE

SPRING HARVEST
Equipping the Church for action

Copyright © 2001 Jani Rubery

First published in 2001 by Spring Harvest Publishing Division
and Paternoster Lifestyle
Reprinted 2002 by Authentic Lifestyle

08 07 06 05 04 03 02 8 7 6 5 4 3 2

Authentic Lifestyle is an imprint of Authentic Media,
P.O. Box 300, Carlisle, Cumbria, CA3 0QS, UK
and P.O. Box 1047, Waynesboro, GA 30830-2047, USA
www.paternoster-publishing.com

The right of Jani Rubery to be
identified as the Author of this Work has been
asserted by her in accordance with the
Copyright, Designs and Patents Act 1988

All rights reserved. No part of this publication may be reproduced, stored in
a retrieval system, or transmitted in any form or by any means, electronic,
mechanical, photocopying, recording or otherwise, without the prior
permission of the publisher or a licence permitting restricted copying. In the
UK such licences are issued by the Copyright Licensing Agency, 90
Tottenham Court Road, London W1P 9HE

Unless otherwise stated, Scripture quotations are taken from the
HOLY BIBLE, NEW INTERNATIONAL VERSION
Copyright © 1973, 1978, 1984 by the International Bible Society.
Used by permission of Hodder and Stoughton Limited. All rights reserved.
'NIV' is a registered trademark of the International Bible Society
UK trademark number 1448790

British Library Cataloguing in Publication Data
A catalogue record for this book is available from the British Library

ISBN 1–85078–430–2

Cover design by Diane Bainbridge
Printed in Great Britain by
Cox & Wyman Ltd, Cardiff Road, Reading

Contents

Introduction

If you've ever met Jani Rubery you'll know that she's the kind of person you'd like to meet if you hadn't met her.

If you've met Jani you'll also know that she's the kind of person you'd like to work with and that she'd be a useful person to have around when the proverbial grenade lands in the foxhole – she'd either throw it back or lie on it.

Jani is no doubt very good at her jobs, but she also seems to be quite good at life, to have retained her joy and her humanity and, in any given month period, her sense of what's really important. This book is one of the first about how to handle the portfolio lifestyle – it isn't written by someone who's made £8 million in two weeks, but it is written by someone whose life is rich and who still knows the names of her children.

Jani's advice is grounded in a strong understanding that all of life can be lived to the glory of God, that, for a Christian, there is no such thing as secular work, and that, though work is important to God, it should never be allowed to become an idol. On these solid foundations, Jani offers practical guidance, both on whether to pursue a 'portfolio' lifestyle and how to handle it if you do. It is, as you can tell by its length, not the last word on the subject, but it is a helpful start by someone who has been there, done that and realises that however successful you are, you don't make princlples out of your

own experience, you make principles out of principles.
Mark Greene
The London Institute for Contemporary Christianity
October 2001

Preface

Having journeyed through my working life attempting to make sense of how I can combine my professional skills with my Christian ministry, I have come to understand that these two worlds can merge together. After trying to discover how I could utilise my skills in the Christian market place, while at the same time being involved in my profession, and with a lot of searching and prayer, the result is that I now live what I and others call a *portfolio lifestyle* – a lifestyle which combines a number of working roles – some paid and some unpaid.

This book is written to share something of my journey. I am not famous nor someone with exceptional skills and talents, just someone who wants to serve the Lord in the most effective way possible and be obedient to his will in my life.

I am a management training consultant, with special emphasis on personal development and leadership training. I spend part of my time working voluntarily as a member of the leadership team of the Salvation Army Mission Team, whose emphasis is on developing young leaders for mission. I attend a Salvation Army Corps in Guildford, Surrey where I also have a leadership role. Married to Clive, who also has a portfolio lifestyle, together we train leaders in the UK and abroad for the Salvation Army. My other role in life has been as stepmother to my two stepchildren – Gillian and Gareth, which I can honestly say has been a privilege.

In writing this book I have drawn on the experience of friends, colleagues and acquaintances who currently are either developing a portfolio lifestyle or are already living it. I thank them for answering my many questions. Specific thanks go to my colleague and friend Adrian Gosling for his invaluable contribution, to my husband Clive for his patience and especially to my editor, Ali Hull – for her patience, experience and most of all, for believing in me.

My prayer is that through sharing my own knowledge and experience as well as what I have learned from others, you will also discover the possibilities of living your life in a way that is not divided between the sacred and the secular, but unified in a constant celebration of, and commitment to, our Saviour, Jesus Christ.

'And whatever you do, whether in word or deed, do it all in the name of the Lord Jesus, giving thanks to God the Father through him.' (Col. 3:17)

1

A Portfolio Lifestyle – What and Why?

Work! Work! Work! is a word which has many different meanings and connotations depending on the context in which we use it. Therefore before we go any further, it is helpful to pause and define what we actually mean when we discuss work in relation to a portfolio lifestyle. The Oxford dictionary definition of work is: 'expenditure of energy, striving, application of effort or exertion to a purpose'.[1] John Stott provides his definition: 'Work is the expenditure of energy (manual or mental or both) in the service of others, which brings fulfilment to the worker, benefit to the community and glory to God.'[2] There is nothing in the pure definition of work that has to do with an office, certain times of day, or specific types of jobs. Many types of activities are regarded as work.

While individuals have always had to combine 'work' and family commitments, the modernisation of employment has created an environment in which many now choose to manage a variety of 'roles', to which they devote their time. The choice to use the word 'roles' is an important one because the word 'work' restricts our thinking into a '9 to 5, going to an office' type of work. We all have a number of roles we fulfil on a daily basis which keep the world going, whether they are paid or unpaid. A portfolio lifestyle is really about roles.

Although we are fulfilling different paid and unpaid roles, whether these be as parent, spouse, boss, teacher, doctor, cleaner, or pilot, we will classify one of these roles as our 'work': most likely the one for which we get paid. Many people work, however, and do not get paid for it. They are combining their family roles with their work roles, spending less time in paid work in order to spend more time at home, perhaps to look after children or elderly relatives. Others are choosing to divide time between paid work and unpaid work for charities or their church.

These are the people who are living what would be described as a portfolio lifestyle - that is, exchanging full-time employment for autonomy. These include homemakers, early retirers, part-time students, part-time pastors, musicians, actors, consultants and the growing number of people who combine paid and unpaid employment. Their working weeks include a variety of jobs and roles, which together create a portfolio of activities. When discussing with a colleague that I was writing a book about portfolio lifestyle, she asked 'What does that mean?' My response was 'It's what you do!' Many people are living a portfolio lifestyle without even knowing it!

This term, *portfolio lifestyle,* is really based on a 1990s trend of an increased desire for independence which has resulted from the 'Boom and Bust' 1980s. It became part of management language when Charles Handy published his book, *The Empty Raincoat,*[3] in 1994, as a response to the problems of choice in which people were finding themselves, when trying to make sense of life and work. However, portfolio lifestyles are not something that began because Charles Handy created the term. This is a trend that has been developing for years.

Let us look at some of the factors that are changing the way people are viewing their work, careers and lifestyle, and are creating what we now know as a portfolio lifestyle.

9 to 5 and all that jazz

For many people, the days of thinking about work in terms of 9 to 5 and structured careers have gone. Recent research has suggested that there is a return to the more individualistic approach to careers that we saw prior to the Industrial Revolution: 'individual, person-centred careers in balance with family and community, less dependent on large bureaucracies'.[4]

An interesting fact is that this whole concept of 9 to 5 is, in historical terms, a fairly new phenomenon. We have somehow come to believe that this concept, of a career that consist of 'working for an organisation 9 to 5', has been around forever. However, when we look at career history we see that for hundreds of years, careers were up to the individual. There were some organisations that could offer structured careers – the church, the military and government, but these were only open to a few. According to *Career Frontiers: New Conceptions of Working Lives:*

> Most people's work was closely tied to their family and community. And although there were no psychologists, sociologists, or careers researchers (that we know of) to report it, there was a certain work-life balance. That is,

those working to live so far outnumbered those living to work that we can be reasonably assured that working lives and personal lives were in synch: they were part and parcel of each other. People were usually artisans, farmers, labourers, or domestic servants, their families were intertwined with their work and their work was intertwined with their community.[5]

It has only been in the last 150 years or so that industrial organisations have emerged and the concept of a career has developed into dependency on an organisation. However, our human desire to grow and achieve remains intact and, in our struggle to survive, individualism is once again emerging as a dominant factor.

This return to the individual taking control of their work life is the result of a number of trends. These include such things as: the change in the shape of organisations from hierarchical to flatter structures; external factors such as market forces; the pace of technological growth; rising standards of living; increase in the amount of travel to workplaces; and the impact of government policy on working practice. The consequences of these changes are having an impact on how people see their careers and their lifestyles as well. These in turn are either pushing or encouraging many into a portfolio lifestyle. Why? Let's look at some of the factors.

Job for life

Where has it gone? There are a number of factors which have resulted in the decline of a 'job for life'. Gone are the days when people felt secure in their jobs, whether they worked in a factory, school, hospital or professional service. Even in the traditionally secure organisations, such as banks and the civil service, there is no promise of a job for life. Also, with the increase in downsizing, a greater focus on profit-making and a volatile commercial environment, there is an increase in mergers, acquisitions and redundancy. In the past we would see this as only a slight possibility. Nowadays it has almost come to be expected at some point in our working lives.

These days an employment contract can look something like this:

> We can't tell you how long we'll be in business.
> We can't promise we won't be bought by another company.
> We can't promise there will be room for promotion.
> We can't promise you a job until retirement.
> We can't promise there will be money for your pension.
> We can't expect your undying loyalty and we aren't sure we want it - and we certainly can't give you ours!

Consequently people are less likely to feel loyal towards their employer. What we are seeing is that people are committed to bosses, colleagues, employees and clients; and even move organisations or places of work based on relationship with people rather than loyalty to an organisation. The principle of 'career' is being replaced with the principle of 'employability'. People are looking to see what they can get from an organisation, rather than what they can give. In fact, in recruitment, some organisations make it very clear from the beginning that 'we will work together as long as you add value to us and we add value to you'.

Traditional promotions

These are also becoming less certain. In the past, when people joined an organisation, they would enquire about the career structure. The response would often be quite clear, with obvious steps up the ladder. Now organisations are less hierarchical, predictable and stable. Structured promotions become less certain, and we hear such statements as 'we can't promise there will be room for promotion'.

As a result, people have to view career mobility differently. If they cannot move up an organisation, because there is less scope to do so, they have to consider taking a new job for a new challenge, perhaps a higher profile, more scope for creativity or an increase in salary. Organisations are responding by providing more flexibility in their compensation packages and developing much wider pay bands, so employees can earn more without necessarily moving up the organisational structure. This makes career paths much more flexible, allowing reduced working hours and fixed-term contracts, which in turn provides a great opportunity for portfolio-style working.

The technology of communication

This is now so sophisticated that it is relatively easy to work at home, with no need for people to be in the workplace. They can be networked into the office and contacted at all times via mobile phones, e-mail, video-links and associated technology. This in turn makes adopting a portfolio working lifestyle much easier because you can now work, literally, from anywhere. The virtual office has arrived!

Mid-career crisis and burn-out

There are other consequences of these changing dynamics. Some people reach a point in their working life where either they do not want the next step, are not offered the next step or there is no next step - a mid-career crisis. It can also happen if people, having worked in one career for a number of years, asks themselves 'Do I want to be doing this for the rest of my life?'

Others reach a point of exhaustion, losing any interest in or motivation for their work. This may happen to those who have been so focused on their careers that they have consistently worked long hours, not taken holidays, ignored relationships and simply neglected their physical and emotional needs. This has become known as burn-out and can, at its worst, result in a physical or emotional breakdown.

Burn-out and mid-career crisis can often be the stimuli which encourage people to re-evaluate their lives, leading to quite significant changes and the achievement of a more balanced lifestyle. The challenge seems to be more about *how* we are using our time rather than *how much* time we use. Many religious denominations are benefiting from this phenomenon by having more people offering to work for the church during mid-life.

These trends have also led to a growth in self-employment. Some of this stems from an entrepreneurial spirit and the increase in the use of technology. Many people, however, have been forced into self-employment through redundancy, bad health or lack of opportunity because of age or family circumstances which require a flexibility that an organisation cannot provide. Successive governments over the past two decades have had a big impact on the trend for self-employment, both through the language they have used when speaking about how to grow the economy, and through government-initiated policies to aid self-employment and small businesses.

I know of individuals who, having been made redundant, have chosen to become consultants, often back into their own industry. Others have bought pubs or started businesses that relate to their hobbies. Yet others have transferred their skills into a supply business for their industry and, of course, many people today are becoming involved in e-commerce.

Sometimes people choose self-employment in order to avoid the increasing amount of stress which they are feeling at work in their organisations. The Institute of Management has estimated that *work-related stress* is responsible for the loss of around £7 billion per annum to British industry through sick leave.[6] One factor which has been identified as causing this rise is an increase in the number of hours people are working. This is affecting both their health and their relationships.

A survey conducted by the Institute of Management in 1999 identified that within five key lifestyle measures, the impact of working long hours were more negative than two years previously.[7]

Impact of Long Hours	1997	1999
	%	%
No time for other interess	77	87
Damaging health	59	71
Affects relationship with children	73	86
Affects relationship with patner	72	79
Reduces productivity over time	55	68

More and more people I meet are questioning the number of hours they are working and the amount of time spent away from home. They are beginning to recognize the impact that long hours have on their health, relationships and even their spirituality. The result is a re-evaluation of the purpose of work, and the nature of their lifestyles. The next generation of workers, according to the Career Innovation Research Group, don't even want to start down the same path. They want to be in control of their destiny.

In 1999 the Career Innovation Research Group (CIRG) conducted a survey of a thousand young professionals from 73 nations. The results showed a shift in how people view their careers, with a definite change in the way people are seeking to balance their work and their lives, so that they `work to live' and do not `live to work'.

> Achieving work-life balance is one of the greatest challenges these people face. Almost all (94%) are willing to work long hours to some extent, but nearly one-fifth of these men and women would like to work part-time and 41% would like more choice over working hours.[8]

When asked to identify their most important 'career values', the top three identified are 'wide horizons', 'work-life balance' and 'professional expertise'. These values are not about loyalty and security. In the past, 'stability' would have come high on the list of career values, whereas in the CIRG survey, this value came at the bottom. There is more of a desire for employability – the ability to maximise personal and professional development in order to ensure they have the skills necessary to remain in work, either with an organisation or self-employed.

These results only affirm what many of us have seen in our own workplaces and lives. We can relate to the effects of the turbulent working environment, the increasing flexibility in career paths and the damaging effects of long working hours. We have also, perhaps, decided that we want more choice and more freedom in our work. These are all factors that may encourage us to consider a portfolio lifestyle. But why should we explore this lifestyle as an option?

Why choose a portfolio lifestyle?

If we adopt a portfolio lifestyle and see our life as a collection of different activities, roles and work opportunities, we can achieve different things. So, for example, you would identify the time which needed to be allocated to necessary activities, such as earning enough for living expenses and looking after your home, and then you have the freedom to decide what to do with the rest of your time, within reason and with God's guidance.

The whole idea of portfolio lifestyle is that it creates options to realise our potential in many different ways. It gives us opportunities to divide our time in a manner which will enable us to serve our churches, communities and families more effectively. For example, working two to three days a week in a well-paid job can free us to use the rest of the time for lower-paid or voluntary work for a church or charity, or to be at home with the family.

There is also the opportunity for using your skills in a variety of ways, rather than believing that your skills do not transfer to any other kind of work, organisation or into your church. For example, expertise acquired as a teacher is highly transferable to other contexts. Organising school journeys and field excursions develops skills that can be used in conference management. Teaching children of differing ages and abilities and delivering assemblies translates into training and presenting to adult audiences. Managing a high school department necessitates the use of standard project management techniques and aspects of human resource management, both of which apply to church work and charity work.

In one sense, portfolio working can also provide more security than that of full-time employment in a large organisation. This is because you rely on a broader base of clients, customers, or industries. You do have to be constantly looking for new opportunities, but it does mean that when the work in one area declines you should be able to find an opportunity somewhere else.

One of the advantages of choosing this lifestyle is that it makes us consider how much money we actually need on which to live. We often believe we need more than we do, but can find there are many things we can do without. Can we drive a more economical car or do without one? Can we shop more economically or have fewer clothes? I have found a new liberty in lowering my expectations for income, and by staying clear of unnecessary financial obligations. The result for me has been more choice and the freedom occasionally to take work that is lower paid or even unpaid.

So portfolio lifestyles can be a positive option for many of us. The reader might ask, 'How do I know if portfolio lifestyle is the appropriate choice?' We understand that this type of lifestyle is not for everyone, but it is still worth exploring your options. You may discover that there are more effective ways of combining your work and spirituality. There may be more options open to you than you think or you might even receive affirmation that you are right where God wants you to be.

Summary

We have explored what portfolio lifestyle is, considered some of the dynamics and their consequences which have had an impact on the development of this type of lifestyle and why it is a positive option. Next we are going to challenge some of the myths that surround how we relate to our work and our faith, and which can stifle our thinking about choice.

[1] J.B. Sykes, Ed., *Concise Oxford Dictionary*, (Oxford: Oxford University Press, 1982)

[2] J. Stott, *Issues Facing Christians Today* (Basingstoke: Marshalls, 1984), p162

[3] Charles Handy, *The Empty Raincoat*, (London: Hutchinson, 1984) p175

[4] M. Peiperl, M. Arthur, R. Goffee, T. Morris (eds.) *Career Frontiers: New Conceptions of Working Lives* (Oxford: Oxford University Press, 2000), p1

[5] M. Peiperl, M. Arthur, R. Goffee, T. Morris (eds.) *Career Frontiers: New Conceptions of Working Lives* (Oxford: Oxford University Press, 2000), p1

[6] Philip Sanders, 'How to get the best from an EAP' (Employee Assistant Programme), *People Management*, 12 October 2000, pp52–53

[7] L. Worrall and C. Cooper, *The Quality of Working Life, 1999 Survey of Managers' Changing Experiences* (Institute of Management)

[8] Jonathan Winter and Charles Jackson, *Riding the Wave*, (Whiteway Research International Ltd, 1999), p4

2

Myths, Truths and Challenges

There are times when we can find we are not doing our best for God, others or ourselves. We may feel as though we are putting energy into the wrong activities and spreading ourselves too thinly. We can feel guilty when we are at work, because we should be putting more time into church and family activities. We can feel guilty because we are putting so much time into church activities that our work and/or our families are being excluded. Many of us often feel these tensions. One of their causes are some of the myths which have been created about how we live out our daily lives in relation to our faith.

Unfortunately, if we believe these myths, they in turn strongly influence the way we live, the choices we make and our peace of mind. It is therefore important to identify and challenge these myths, in order to open our minds to the possibilities of living our lives in a more creative and fulfilling way than we may think possible at the moment. I have identified four myths which I believe can become barriers, stopping us not only from thinking more widely about our lives, but also specifically preventing us from considering a portfolio lifestyle as an option.

Myth 1: Our secular work can have no relation to our Christian ministry.

This myth stems from the belief that there is a divide between the sacred and the secular. There is still a peculiar dualism which exhibits itself in the view that somehow what we do from Monday to Friday is divorced from what we do on a Sunday. This is truly a myth which needs to be shattered but, unfortunately, the church has tended to perpetuate it. In many parts of the Christian church, a hierarchy of ministry has developed which leads us to believe that if we are in 'full-time' church ministry – for example, as a pastor, youth worker, etc., then we are the most spiritual of Christians. Being missionaries also suggests a superior spirituality. The implication is that if we have chosen to live out our life in the workplace, we have chosen a worldly option – once we get our spirituality sorted out, we will make the right choice and begin 'proper' ministry – in the church.

You may argue that the church does not explicitly teach this, but I have found this belief, however it has been taught, in the attitudes people adopt, their behaviour and the statements they make. A colleague of mine, Adrian, had taught for ten years in a comprehensive school where each day he would interact with hundreds of individuals, most of whom had no understanding of Jesus. After a hard but fulfilling week of teaching he would often go to church on Sunday, where he would see the 'missionary map' on the noticeboard. There he would see the names and localities of those who had been sent out from the church to take on Christian ministry in a variety of exotic and less exotic areas. Unfortunately his own work in a medium-sized suburban town did not qualify Adrian for a posting on the world map. When he gave up teaching full-time, however, and spent his week both teaching and working for the Salvation Army's Mission Team, then his name did appear. Even then, it was his work with the mission team that was mentioned on the map. Teaching secondary school students in Watford did not, it seems, qualify as 'mission'. And which teachers does the church pray for – those who work all week in the schools or those who teach in Sunday School? Surely it should be both.

Truth: Our lives should be a constant ministry which glorifies God, no matter in what context we are working.
'And whatever you do, whether in word or deed, do it all in the name of the Lord Jesus, giving thanks to God the Father through him' (Col. 3:17).

Scripture does not teach us that we are only to glorify God when we are in the church, when we are meeting with our brothers and sisters in Christ, or when we are preaching and teaching. We are told that whatever we do, we do it for the glory of God. In order to do this we need to develop *lay theology*. 'Lay theology has sought to emphasise the importance of every Christian both in the church and in the world and the need for each person to fashion a thoughtful Christian perspective on every activity.'[1] It is not the purpose of this book to explore this theology, but we do have a responsibility to understand biblical principles in order to ensure that our faith and work merge together so that we bring glory to God in all that we do.

One of the greatest ways we bring our faith into our work is, of course, through evangelism. As an itinerant worker, it was very difficult for me to see how my work could possibly be part of my ministry. I then discovered that through building relationships with my colleagues, even though I saw them infrequently, I was able to start sharing my faith and eventually some of them came to faith themselves. In recent days, I have been discovering that even the gift of prophecy can be used in the times when I am doing one-to-one coaching. Gifts of encouragement can be utilised effectively in workplaces where discouragement is frequent. Pastoral gifts can be applied in our service to colleagues in the office as well as friends at church. We often box up our spiritual gifts and believe that they are for Sundays only. Why would God give us gifts which are only to be used within the confines of what we call 'church'?

Furthermore, just as we confine our spiritual gifts to the church, we confine our 'secular' skills to the workplace and don't offer them to the church. It can be difficult to see how our everyday working skills can be used for 'Christian' ministry. Perhaps it may seem easy for someone who is a nurse and who also wants to do missionary work abroad. If you are a warehouse manager, however, it might be more difficult to identify skills which are transferable to other contexts, although not impossible.

When I was initially invited to work for the evangelist Phil Wall, then the leader of the Salvation Army Mission Team, it was hard for me to see what skills I could bring to a group of people whose main purpose was evangelism. I had no training in evangelism and felt no call to full-time ministry. I discovered, however, that I could bring to the team my expertise in training and developing others, team-building and leadership skills. These were elements that were needed as the team was developing, in scope as well as numbers.

As a teacher with middle-management responsibility, Adrian had developed a range of organisational, administrative and supervisory skills in addition to an understanding of effective communication. Any secondary school teacher will have massive experience of applying attention to detail in a fast-moving environment, amounting to a set of transferable skills which can be applied in many contexts. Adrian was able to use these skills in a role within the Salvation Army Mission Team, developing processes for event management and project implementation.

Everything we do within our daily lives – be that taking children to school, making government policy, pastoring a congregation, managing people in an office, teaching students – it can all be done in the name of Jesus and giving the glory to God.

'So whether you eat or drink or whatever you do, do it all for the glory of God' (1 Cor. 10:31).

Challenge: List the skills, talents and gifts you use at work that you could bring to the church. List the skills, talents and gifts you use in your church that you could bring to your work.

Myth 2: My work could not possibly be God's calling.

How can shuffling papers at an office give glory to God? How can selling car insurance give glory to God? How can teaching people computer skills give glory to God? How can being a psychologist bring glory to God? How can being an artist bring glory to God?

Jonathan Edwards, the triple jump Olympic gold medallist, says, 'I jump into a sandpit for a living. Am I doing anything worthwhile here? The pointlessness of it.

You see doctors in Rwanda and think, "They're making a difference, but I'm jumping into a sandpit. Who benefits from that?"[2] In the biography, *A Time to Jump*, Jonathan reflects upon the challenges of answering this question and describes the searching he had to go through to discover that even jumping into a sandpit can be a calling from God.

After losing out on a medal in the Barcelona Olympics in 1992 he says, 'It was terribly hard for me to admit to myself, but I began to realise that huge part of me was only in it for me, for selfish reasons.'[3] He then went on to jump at a Grand Prix final in Turin and it was there that his story takes a turn. 'On that runway in Turin I rediscovered my focus and told myself, "I'm doing this for God. I could be the worst triple jumper the world has ever seen, but this is what I'm going to do… It was a fundamental moment for me as a Christian, in terms of having something very strong inside me broken. Whatever desire for success, recognition, that I had, and all stated as a desire to serve God, had been challenged in a very painful and traumatic way. I think God was disciplining me at those Olympics, not to punish me but to bring me closer to him.'[4]

The issue for Jonathan, as for many of us, is not that our work is not our calling, but that we don't recognise it as such. We need a 'wake up' call to remind us who is in control, who gives us our gifts and skills, and for whom we are really working.

Truth: God calls people to many different kinds of work.

From the beginning of time we see examples of God calling people to a variety of work roles. We see this in the story of the building of the tabernacle in Exodus:

19

Moses said to the Israelites, "See the Lord has chosen Bezalel son of Uri, the son of Hur, of the tribe of Judah, and he has filled him with the Spirit of God, with skill, ability and knowledge in all kinds of craftsmanship... And he has given both him and Oholiab, son of Ahisamach, of the tribe of Dan, the ability to teach others... So Bezalel, Oholiab and every skilled person to whom the Lord has given skill and ability to know how to carry out all the work of constructing the sanctuary are to do the work just as the Lord has commanded (Ex. 35:30-36:1).

Just as God called and anointed people for the building of the tabernacle, as well as David, Nehemiah, Daniel, Matthew – the list is endless – so too he calls and anoints us for the work in his world today. We have the misconception that God's world is the church and we forget that everything in the world is God's creation. Our office blocks, hospitals, government buildings, houses and streets are all God's creation, ruled by him and ordained by him. So why wouldn't God call us to be involved in every part of his world? Why would he not want us to be fulfilling our ministries in all aspects of society, whether in parenting, working in the community, government, professional occupations, administration, health services or the hundreds of other occupations in society?

Lesslie Newbiggin, in his book *Trinitarian Doctrine for Today's Mission*, cites a speech given by Canon Warren at a world missionary conference in 1952:

I believe there is a call for an entirely new type of missionary activity to be developed alongside the traditional modes. We need, for instance, to envisage men and women of scientific training who will be ready to give their service in development schemes, going to their work as ordinary salaried officials and bringing their expert knowledge to bear on some local situation. But they will go, not merely as those whose Christian convictions are marginal to their work, as is commonly the case of many today. Rather they will go with a vocation consciously and deliberately to seek to work out 'a disciplined and purified technology' in the light of Christian insights.[5]

Amazingly, this was preached in 1952 and we are still struggling along in the church, not recognising that vocation can be in the church or outside the church. The conclusion is clear. All work can be God's calling. We need to acknowledge this truth and act accordingly. It is also important to recognise that no work is more important than any other – our responsibility is to be obedient to the will of God and serve him in the place in which he puts us.

'Each one should retain the place in life that the Lord assigned to him and to which God has called him. This is the rule I lay down in all the churches... Brothers, each man, as responsible to God, should remain in the situation God called him to.' (1 Cor. 7:17, 24)

Challenge: What are the elements of your work which can be considered part of your ministry: for example, which parts of your work serve others? What do you do that assists colleagues, develops others, helps healing, brings encouragement, has a positive impact on society or the environment? Are there more ways you can bring ministry into your work?

Myth 3: Money is evil.

You may wonder why I would choose to highlight this myth. It is because both for myself and others I have counselled on the issue of portfolio lifestyle, I have found the issue of wealth can be a major problem, preventing people from seeing the possibilities of creating an alternative way of living.

The subject of money is one which causes many debates within the Christian community. One reason is that money is an emotive subject, touching the hearts of many, stirring such strong feelings that some avoid approaching it at all. Opinions on it are based on deep-rooted values and beliefs, instilled in us by our families, the Bible and the teaching of our denomination. These influences may have helped us develop our own belief system about wealth — or they may have totally confused us.

While some churches don't even teach at all on the subject of work or money, other churches have a distorted teaching. Some teach that money is a sign of God's blessing and therefore poverty is a sign of his displeasure. Others teach that money is evil and therefore, in order to be spiritual, we need to live a life of poverty. There are many biblical references warning us of the dangers of a love of money, which back up this second position. For good reason, Jesus needs to remind us of our potential for greed, bad stewardship, and idolatry, and as with all Scripture, these are the guidelines by which we develop our lifestyles.

The challenge is that there are many, for whatever reasons, who are in situations which give them the opportunity to earn a lot of money. To some this is seen as being inconsistent with Scripture. This view has created a guilt complex amongst many Christians who have well-paid jobs. Not only do they feel guilty, but they are often criticised by people in their church and are sometimes accused of making money their idol. While it cannot be denied that wealth can become an idol, and an obstacle between us and God, so can many other things, including our families, television, status or success.

Truth: Money in itself is no more evil than anything else by which we can be seduced. The main issue is whether or not we allow our wealth to become more important than our relationship with our Lord.

Richard Foster, in *Money, Sex and Power* [6], uses the terms 'dark side' and 'light side' to describe the dichotomy of the wealth issue. Just as the Bible teaches us about the 'dark side' of wealth, there are also the examples of when God shows that wealth is a blessing he gives which can even enhance our relationship with him. 'When God gives any man wealth and possessions, and enables him to enjoy them, to accept his lot and be happy in his work – this is a gift from God' (Ecc. 5:19).

We are not to shy away from being called into vocations which result in wealth. Richard Foster emphasises this point::

> Christians are to immerse themselves in the world of capital and business. This is a high and holy calling. It is a good thing for those under the rule of God to make money. We should not hide from these opportunities to labour for the sake of the kingdom of God. Believers can and should be called into positions of power, wealth and influence. It is a spiritual calling to take leadership roles in government,

education, and business. Some are called to make money – lots of money – for the glory of God and the larger public good.[7]

Foster goes on to discuss how important it is for there to be teaching and discipline with regards to possessing money without being possessed by it: the discipline of learning how to own things without treasuring them.

It may seem as though consideration of this particular myth about wealth has taken us off course. This issue can, however, be a real problem for many Christians as they endeavour to live out a fulfilling, vocational life in Christ. Ultimately, this can prevent people from making choices about working shorter hours, working for charity organisations which pay less, or working voluntarily. I have to come to realise that fulfilment is not about the amount of money I earn, but about doing what God has called me to do, with the talents he has given me to do it. Fulfilment is about enjoying my work because it is what God specifically designed me to do. Letting go of a desire for a greater income can lead to a greater quality of living.

On the other hand, wealth can become a problem if you are in a position which does allow you to make money or create wealth. If you are struggling with the guilt of this, for whatever reasons, this can prevent you not only from celebrating your wealth, but can also limit you in sharing your wealth appropriately. This has been an issue which I have had to work through with my husband. Through prayer and asking others to help us be accountable we have learned to accept the reality that we work in a well-paid profession which means we have the freedom to give more of our time voluntarily as well as share our wealth with others.

Whatever our circumstances are with regards to wealth, we have to constantly remind ourselves that the wealth is not ours – it is a gift from God.

> You may say to yourself, `My power and the strength of my hands have produced this wealth for me.' But remember the Lord your God, for it is he who gives you the ability to produce wealth, and so confirms his covenant, which he swore to your forefathers, as it is today (Deut. 8:17-18).

Challenge: Are you finding the issue of wealth has become a burden for you, either because you have it or because of your fear of not having it? If so, identify the reasons why and find someone to talk and pray through this issue with you.

Myth 4: I have no freedom of choice.

Many people are inclined to think negatively about their working lives, convincing themselves that there are a whole range of barriers to their personal choices. These barriers may have developed from their family role models, such as a father staying in a job forever or mother who was never in paid work. They may have developed through beliefs about what others expect from them – family, church, colleagues, society. Some of us will also have been influenced through the theological teaching of our denomination on issues of choice and free will.

When counselling I have heard such statements as:
- I cannot change jobs because I do not have transferable skills – I would have to take a demotion or pay cut.

● I cannot work from home because my employer is not flexible.

● Going self-employed is too risky.

● I cannot live on less money because of my mortgage and car payments.

● I must stay at home to look after the children because this is what is expected of me.

● My organisation will never let me work reduced or flexible hours, there is no precedent.

● I cannot make any changes until God tells me to.

In reality we do have choice, but it is sometimes difficult to see this and we can be determined to believe that there is no way we are able to change our job, career or any other aspect of our lives. We look at the impossibilities rather than the possibilities that could facilitate change, whether these are the option of working from home, becoming self-employed, or accepting more flexible modes of employment. We raise objections when presented with opportunities for change, perhaps arguing that we *must* stay at home to look after the children or that we *should* remain committed to our present employer.

Individuals sometimes suggest that their lack of choice is a form of divine determinism. 'God is making me do this!' God may have given us clear direction as to what he wants us to do, but we still have the choice as to whether or not we do it. The concept of free will is an underlying theme of our Christian faith.

Truth: We do have freedom. No one can coerce us to do anything, and God chooses not to. This may be a hard truth to swallow, but it cannot be denied.

Responsibility rests with us and we must make choices.

It is very easy to be trapped into believing that we have no alternatives. We can convince ourselves that we are forced into all of the situations we find ourselves. The author's personal experiences serve to illustrate the nature of this cul-de-sac mentality. When God began challenging me about 'giving up' some of what I believed to be my 'normal work' (i.e. teaching and training) in order to give my time, skills and energy to 'church' work, it was easy to come up with reasons why this was not a viable option.

I believed that if I started turning down consulting contracts that I would be left out of the 'network' and I would not be asked to do *any* contracts! In fact, through being faithful to God and saying 'no' to some of the contracts, in order to devote time to my work with the Salvation Army, God opened doors to new fruitful consulting opportunities – both in challenge and financial terms. This meant I was enjoying my consulting, while at the same time I had the time and financial means to devote to my work with the Salvation Army.

It is easy to think that employers will not want their employees suddenly going part-time in order to pursue a portfolio lifestyle, but a surprising number of people have found that approaching their organisation with a well-thought out, properly costed plan to do just that can be met with favour. There has to be some advantage for the company as well as the individual, and it would be wrong to suggest that all employers will look favourably on such suggestions. But equally it would be wrong to say that all employers will say 'No'. Employers can sometimes be more flexible than we expect.

Not only has it been difficult for me to challenge the 'I have no choice' syndrome, but in our mission to facilitate others in discovering their vocation I have met many people who also find this a struggle.

When counselling people who are unhappy in their work, here is a sample of a typical conversation when they are asked the question, 'Why don't you leave?'

Response: 'I have no choice.'
Question: 'Why don't you have a choice?'
Response: 'Because I have to pay my mortgage.'
Question: 'Why do you have to pay the mortgage?'
Response: 'Because I have to have a house to live in.'
Question: 'Why do you have to have a house to live in?'
Response: 'Because my family has to have somewhere to live.'
Question: 'Do you *have* to buy a house to have somewhere to live?'
   'Do you *have* to live in that particular area?'
   'Do you *have* to live in a home that large?'
Response: 'No.'
Question: 'So you could choose to rent, move to a cheaper area or a smaller home?'
Response: 'Yes.'

We always have some choices, even if we don't perceive them. For example, when challenged about the statements, 'I must stay at home' or 'I cannot leave my job', we can discover that we like staying at home or like the people we work with. We may believe it is important that a parent be at home with the children and we would therefore not choose to do anything else. One of our values may be loyalty to an employer and this would override any other desire to change jobs. We discover we are actually making choices – and making those choices for a wide variety of reasons.

Of course, some people cannot escape from the various constraints under which they live, whether these are physical or psychological, religious or institutional, economic or political. We should recognise, however, that even within these constraints we can still enjoy spiritual, mental and relational freedom. Remember, the concept of free will is foundational to our Christian faith. Even given certain parameters, individuals can still work toward greater freedom in their spiritual development, intellectual progress and relationships. Secure in the knowledge that not all depends on their own efforts, they know that whether they succeed or fail, ultimately there awaits them the full liberty of the Kingdom of God.

Challenge: Write down all the situations where you perceive you have 'no choice', for instance: within your job, home, work, family commitments, social commitments. Now ask yourself a series of questions, similar to those listed above – why do I feel I have to do this? Why do I think this? Is this really true? What are the alternatives? You will discover you have more choices than you initially thought.

Summary

There are so many unhelpful beliefs and attitudes which prevent us from understanding God's will for our lives. I have identified those which I feel have been hindrances for myself and others I have met on a similar journey. It has been important to acknowledge these challenges in order to bring down the barriers that could prevent you from taking the next steps in the journey: of exploring the possibilities of creating a life which is fulfilling for you and is in accordance with God's will for your life.

The next step of the journey will be to explore how we discover our vocation and whether a portfolio lifestyle would be complementary to that vocation.

---

[1] Robert Banks, *The Business of Life* (Oxford: Lion Publishing, 1980), p417

[2] Malcolm Folley, *A Time to Jump*, (London: HarperCollins, 2000), p143

[3] Malcolm Folley, *A Time to Jump*, p89

[4] Malcolm Folley, *A Time to Jump*, p90

[5] Lesslie Newbiggin, *Trinitarian Doctrine for Today's Mission* (Paternoster, 1998), p66

[6] Richard Foster, *Money, Sex and Power* (London: Hodder and Stoughton, 1985) – summary of Chapter 3, pp37–50

[7] Richard Foster, *Money, Sex and Power*, pp45–46

3

Discovering Vocation

Where am I? How did I get here? Where should I be?
How many of us have been lost, not in the place we
thought we should be? We have set off on a journey without preparing, not looking at the map, nor asking for guidance. This can make for an exciting journey, but more
often involves frustration, loss of time or even failure to
arrive at the planned destination.

This is not only true for getting from place to place
geographically, but also for planning our lives. We
progress on our journey without making a plan or asking
for guidance. We don't look out for the signposts and sig-
nals we get on the way, nor do we stop and ask others for
directions. Eventually we end up somewhere and we
don't know how we got there. At this point we have to
stop and ask, 'Where am I? How did I get here?' We may
like where our journey has taken us, which is good. On
the other hand, we may not, and that is not a good place
to be.

There is a variety of reasons why this happens. I classify
these into what I call *games people play*. There are a number of games that are played as people journey through
their working life. We play them because that is an easier
option than having to consider our journey. Game-playing

helps us avoid responsibility: we can blame other people or our circumstances when things go wrong.

First of all there is the *waiting game* – waiting for Prince Charming. One day it will happen: the perfect job will come along. God will open the right door. He might, of course, but sometimes he also wants us to do some knocking. We say things like: 'It will be different when…' 'If I wait long enough, things will change…' 'If I wait long enough the day will come when I'll find fulfilment.' These are all examples of the waiting game. The trouble is, the waiting game can go on for a very long time.

The *pinball game* is another game we play. We take a shot at something and if it doesn't work, we rebound into something else. We continue this game, sometimes winning and sometimes losing, but never really getting very far or feeling very satisfied.

We may also play the *interesting jobs* game. We see a job or profession that seems to be 'interesting'. It may prove to be so, but this can wear off and we get bored. We then move on to the next 'interesting' type of work. Eventually we tally up a whole series of interesting jobs which do not necessarily fit together and we may feel as though we have not achieved anything and are unsure where to go next.

The good news is that sometimes these games end up working for us! We can look back and see that the skills we have developed and the experiences we have had were never wasted. I say this as a person who has been a cleaning maid, waitress, secretary, aerobics instructor, personnel manager and consultant. I can see how each of these jobs has helped me, particularly in building my interpersonal skills, which are now crucial to everything I do. The challenge comes when these games do not end. There needs to be a point when we start to define the general direction and purpose of our journey, our vocation. It's never too late!

This definition will be different for each one of us. For some of us the direction and purpose is very defined. Perhaps we have heard from God very clearly, either while praying by ourselves or through studying God's word. Others may be sure about their purpose and their general direction, at least for the moment, but are not so certain of the specifics of how they are going to get there. Others may know the direction but are unsure about the purpose. God has the answers to these gaps in our understanding. My experience, however, is that God does not give us all the answers at once, but if we ask, he does reveal each step at the appropriate time.

Even if we know where we are going, it will not be smooth sailing with everything going according to plan. Rather, if we can find the direction we need to go and discover what is meant to be our vocation – through understanding ourselves and God's will in our lives – we will at least be on a journey which is fulfilling, even if the route is not always clear. We also need to recognize that, of course, God reserves the right to change the plan at any time.

What is vocation?

Thus far I have been using the word 'vocation' without offering a definition of what I mean. I use the word vocation quite deliberately. A vocation is much more than just a job – teaching, journalism, managing, being a nurse, musician, minister, and so on. The word vocation is derived from the Latin word *vocatio*, which means 'to call'. 'Vocation is our divinely given life-purpose embracing all dimensions of our human existence and the special dimensions of service Christians undertake in the church and world.'[1]

We are reminded by Paul in his letter to the Ephesians, 'I urge you to live a life worthy of the calling you have received' (Eph. 4:1). He is not just writing this to the church leaders, but to everyone. The challenge is that vocation and calling in Christian circles are normally used about specific types of work, such as full-time church ministry, health professions or youth work. In chapters 4-6 of his letter to the Ephesians, however, Paul goes on to describe some of the contexts in which we are called to live as Christ's people: congregational life, marriage, home, workplace and society.

A Christian vocation is about much more than a job or profession. It is about living for the praise and glory of the Lord and serving God's purposes in every context of life. Whereas a career is about one part of our life, vocation embraces our whole life. So when I talk about discovering my vocation, it is more than just finding the right job. It is about discovering God's purpose in my occupation, church, family and community. God does not just have a wonderful plan for our lives: he has a purpose. To take this one step further we must remember that 'a career is chosen but a calling is accepted'.[2]

This is why I believe a portfolio lifestyle can be so responsive to God's command. It does not limit us to thinking about our lives in separate boxes, but embraces all aspects of living and enables us to understand our whole lives as a calling. The challenge, of course, is how to discover what it is. I have been involved in vocational guidance, both professionally and within the Salvation Army, and have developed a helpful process for people to discover their vocation by examining: where have they been; where are they now; and where are they going.

The rest of this chapter is designed to provide you with practical help. I have developed some specific methods and tools based on my experience, which I will include in the next sections.[3] I hope that through this process you will gain a better understanding of your strengths, weaknesses, skills, values and passions. This in turn should help you build a picture of how to move into the future. This is a detailed process and you may find it helpful to respond to each question as it is posed, before proceeding to the next section.

Where Have I Been?

The first step in discovering where we want to go is examining where we have been. It is important to think about our past and realise the impact our personal history has had on the development of our character. It will also have affected the choices we have made or perhaps the choices that have been made for us. This, in turn, will have had an impact on the way we view our lives, careers and vocations.

There are two good reasons for exploring the critical events, situations and people from our past. Firstly, so that we can understand more about why we are as we are, by seeing the patterns that have developed in our lives: those activities, roles and lifestyle choices which seem to be consistent throughout our life. Secondly, by identifying and understanding these patterns, we can then move on to challenging them. We can try to discern which of these patterns are helpful and should be continued and which patterns are unhelpful and should cease.

In order to reveal these patterns we need to identify the *situations and people* that have had an impact on us. Who are the people whose behaviour, teaching and relationships have most influenced our values, beliefs and attitudes? They could be family members such as parents, grandparents, aunts or uncles, or perhaps a teacher who either encouraged or disciplined us in a way that helped in our personal or educational development. Maybe we can recall a significant sports coach, Sunday school teacher, minister or spiritual mentor. We will all have at least one person, but probably a combination of several people, who have helped shape our development. It is important to identify them in order to understand who our role models have been. They will have had a tremendous impact on how we view the world and the choices we make.

For example, I had a female professor at University who encouraged me to be successful in a 'man's' world. There is no doubt she had an impact on how I have viewed my choices. Instead of being put off certain jobs because I saw them as being only for men, my belief was and is that being a woman should not prevent me from using the mind, gifts or talents which God has given me. Consequently, my first job out of university was with an oil company. I was a female personnel officer in a male-dominated industry – there were not many women in an oil field, not even in Wyoming! Had I not been mentored by this professor, I would not have had the confidence to take this job.

Challenge: Who have been the significant people in your life?

Another way of identifying these patterns is to reflect back on the subjects which you *really* liked during your education. Notice the emphasis: not necessarily the subjects you chose to take but the ones you enjoyed and from which you gained encouragement. For some it might have been the black-and-white subjects, such as the sciences and maths. Others might have preferred English, sociology or psychology, or maybe the creative sphere – music, drama or art. I meet many people who feel that their education did not involve them in following the subjects they enjoyed. Perhaps this was due to pressure from their educational institutions to take subjects that were acceptable in order to 'get on' in the education system, or it could have been parental coercion to follow in their footsteps. Sometimes people even chose subjects based on what their friends had chosen. It is important to identify those subjects you enjoyed, not just those that you studied or were good at. This will give you a better understanding of what really motivates you.

Challenge: List the subjects you really enjoyed during your education. If there were none, identify those subjects you would have enjoyed if they had been on offer.

As we think about our education it is also helpful to reflect back on **what types of activities and roles** we enjoyed during our school years. Think about the clubs, sports and organisations which you chose to join. Why did you belong to them? Was it interest, skill or because of friends? What role did you play in these groups – were you always the organiser, secretary or leader, or did you just enjoy the social aspect? Maybe you were a rebel in the group or maybe you were the House Captain or Form Prefect (president of the class for Americans reading this book). Maybe you were a performer in music, dance or drama.

The types of roles and activities in which we took part during our 'younger' years will definitely have had an impact on the roles and activities in which we get involved later in life. Psychologists suggest that our personality is more or less developed by our early teen years. Therefore, exploring the things we liked and disliked during our developing years will provide a good indication of what we are likely to continue to like and dislike in our adult years. This may show itself in different ways: for instance, rather than being the captain of the school cricket team, you are now a manager, a leader in your local church, or perhaps captain of the golf team or a local councillor.

For me, going through this process of thinking about roles and activities growing up initially brought embarrassment. Reflecting back on my life, I realised that I had always been in areas of 'performing'. I started dancing when I was five and continued to dance until I was eighteen. I was a cheerleader (hard to admit, but true) for six years, and I was a twirler in the marching band (another admission), both of which are performing roles. I always found myself in leadership positions, whether it was captain of the gymnastics team, head cheerleader, or being president of my sorority at University. Although it was challenging to recognise that I liked performing and being in leadership, it also helped me understand that this is part of my character and, bar transformation by God, is likely to remain so. The exciting part is that, through understanding myself and through God's guidance, I have been able to find a vocation where my skills and experience can be used together with my performing skills: management training, Christian teaching and local church leadership. Others have different natures and talents, which can make them prefer different types of working lifestyles – for instance, working alone or working as part of a team.

Challenge: Identify the roles and activities in which you were involved during your 'developing' years. What impact have they had your roles and activities today?

Another important aspect of understanding our life patterns is distinguishing *life events* which have shaped who we are. These are events or situations which have had an influence on our choices and priorities. For example, moving home or schools often will have an impact on how we react to change. Some may continue this pattern and constantly feel the need to move home, job or even church. I met a Salvation Army officer recently who was the daughter of missionary parents. Now living in Costa Rica, she has been so used to moving countries that, not surprisingly, she has chosen to apply for missionary service herself. Others react in the opposite way, trying to avoid change at all costs. I have also met the grown-up children of Salvation Army officers who have not moved since their early twenties. Frequently staying in the same occupation all their working lives, they often say they don't want their children to have to experience the disruption of moving every two to three years.

Divorce, adoption and even abuse will, for some, have had an influence on how they make their choices about work and lifestyle. The need for security is known to be stronger in those that come from families affected by these particular issues. My step-daughter says that her parents' divorce has made relationships very important to her. Gill values being part of a team and only likes working in an environment which provides her with the security of genuine relationships. A colleague of mine, who comes from an abusive background, has told me that, for him, it created a strong need for survival. This has led to a drive for success which in turn has influenced many of the choices he has made.

Conversely, my son-in-law comes from a background of security, recognition and support. His parents have worked for most of their lives in the same kind of employment, and lived in the same area. Chris is a human factors practitioner with the Defence Evaluation Research Agency (DERA). When I asked him why he chose to work in the civil service rather than a consultancy, he replied that he wanted to work in an environment that provided him with the security and support he was used to. Now that DERA is privatised, this has caused Chris and his colleagues a tremendous amount of anxiety, because the security that they thought they had is being threatened. Many of them are leaving for more secure positions, because they are the type of people who choose organisations which provide structure and security.

For myself, growing up in a family affected by alcoholism has had an impact on the lifestyle choices I have made. One of the biggest influences of this kind of background is that it creates a lack of trust in others. The result for me is that I am very individualistic, which is probably why most of my working life I have been self-employed and am very happy as a consultant.

There are a whole variety of life-events which will have affected each one of us. We each have a different story to tell, but the reality is we do each have a story. It is important to think about our story and understand the impact these events will have had and the way they have influenced us to make our choices or take particular paths.

Challenge: Which life-events can you distinguish which are likely to have had a major influence on your lifestyle patterns?

The size and type of family we grew up in will have had an impact on our life patterns. Birth order is known to have an effect on personality development, and research has shown that first children are more likely to desire structured environments which they can control. Some research suggests that a large percentage of leaders are first children. There is also evidence that children of larger families are more likely to enjoy working in groups and being part of a 'family' environment.[4]

The *parents' occupations* can also have an influence. If parents have been in high-profile, high-status roles, children often tend to follow in their footsteps. Sometimes children follow their parents into professions such as the military, medicine, and even church ministry. This is not always true, of course, and sometimes children will purposely rebel against their parents' occupations. Paradoxically, even this is still a response to their parents.

At first glance, you would think this is the case in my family, where my step-son has been brought up by two people who are involved in the world of business – both management training consultants with business backgrounds. Gareth has chosen a musical vocation – which, when examined more closely, is not unlike his parental role models – he is still performing, albeit in a different way. He will probably end up with a portfolio lifestyle like many musicians (and his parents). So initially his choices could appear as rebellion against the traditional business, middle-class working life. In reality, however, the motivations are similar – independence and performing – it is just the context and arena which are different.

Challenge: What impact, if any, do you think your parents' occupations have had on you and the lifestyle choices you have made?

Wealth – having it, or the lack of it – will also affect the choices we make. For some, childhood poverty can become a major driving force in later life, and they will constantly seek to ensure that they are never poor again. This can prevent them from ever considering a job for the enjoyment they might get out of it, because money has become the only criterion that matters. Most people, however, work for a mixture of motives: for pleasure in what they are doing and for the payment that enables them to support themselves and their families.

Challenge: What have been the family influences which will have affected the way you view work and money?

I have just outlined some of the factors from the past which can influence the patterns of lifestyle which we develop. I have posed some questions which I hope will help you identify some of those influences for yourselves. There will be others and a helpful method of discovering them, by producing a picture of your past, is to draw what is known as a life-line or life-tree. Take a blank sheet of paper and draw a line either vertically or horizontally. Start at the beginning of your life and make a branch for each significant event, person and stage which you believe has had an impact on you. This will help you see the patterns which have developed. Continue this process until you get to your current position. You can include dates and years, if you find that helpful.

For example, recall my example about performing and leadership. When I drew my life-tree I saw how many branches had to do with performing or leadership. Obviously there are a number of branches not shown in my example, but I wanted to demonstrate how the leadership and performing theme developed in my life. So I ended up with something that looks like this:

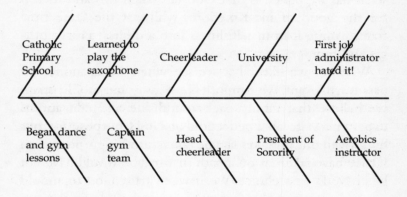

Catholic Primary School | Learned to play the saxophone | Cheerleader | University | First job administrator hated it!

Began dance and gym lessons | Captain gym team | Head cheerleader | President of Sorority | Aerobics instructor

This is just a brief sample but will hopefully give an idea of the process. Once you have completed your tree, leave it and then come back to it. You will, no doubt, have forgotten either a person or event, so add to it as you remember. Then examine the patterns of the events and people which you found to be significant. Are there any recurrent themes? Have you frequently changed from one thing to another, moved a lot, preferred solo activities or being with a group, held leadership positions? Identifying these patterns will help you see the trends of your life, many of which will continue into the future.

At this point, the question should be asked, 'Does spirituality come into this?' The answer is that it must, although when and where will be different for each of us. What we do know is that God takes as we are – warts and all – and creates something beautiful, once we have become Christians. For example, as previously described, I found it difficult to discover how important public recognition had been in my life. When I became a Christian in my late twenties, this desire did not suddenly disappear. Instead what has happened is that God has taken this and used it for the good of his Kingdom, whilst at the same time transforming it from selfishness into a desire to serve others and him.

Whether we like what we see when we examine our past is irrelevant. We cannot take it away, but as Christians we believe that family background, life and educational experiences are all a reflection of God's purpose for our lives. Even our mistakes can be taken into his purpose, even if they have taken us on a path that maybe would have not been God's first choice. We have to trust God to mould these experiences into something worthwhile so that we can serve him in the best way possible.

This brings us to the end of Stage 1 – analysing the past – where have I been? The next stage is analysing the present – where am I now?

Where am I now?

This stage involves assessing your present position. What are your *skills*: are they manual, intellectual, administrative, artistic, selling, teaching?

What *experience* do you have? What types of jobs and roles have you had to date? What did you enjoy about them? What did you dislike about them?

What *activities and roles* motivate you? Do you like to be in a stable, structured environment or do you prefer flexibility and creativity? Do you like to be clear about what you are doing on a day-to-day basis or do you like variety? Do you prefer working on your own or with others? The worksheet in Appendix A will help you identify what skills and activities you prefer or you may just want to start with a blank sheet and brainstorm these for yourself.

What *values* have you identified as being important in your life? What are those principles or standards to which you would hold: for example, time with family, integrity, independence, risk, variety? It is important to identify your values in order to make choices in line with your beliefs. The questionnaire in Appendix B may help you establish your values in relation to work and will guide you in your thinking. Once again, you may want to begin with a blank sheet, and brainstorm.

It is also important to consider the *constraints* in your life. What kind of personality do you have? For example, if you are the kind of person who needs security and structure, you need to work in an environment that provides that. What are your skills and gifts? If you are not a skilled musician, you cannot make a career out of music! Do you have children? Do you need to work within a short travelling distance? What amount of money do you need to live on? It is critical to outline these constraints to help you to be comprehensive in the choices you make for your lifestyle. As discussed in chapter one, it is important to not limit our choices while at the same time we have to be realistic about the constraints under which we must live.

It is also crucial to identify the **key relationships** which are important to you, to ensure that these are included in your planning for the future. These will include family, church members, friends, mentors, and those you might be discipling.

So many questions! You may find it helpful to answer each of these questions in turn by taking a blank piece of paper and listing your response under each category, as well as using the questionnaires in Appendices A and B. Another helpful exercise is to take a blank piece of paper and draw a picture of where you see yourself now – using only images. This is an amazing tool to use, as images often speak louder than words about how we feel and about where we are.

By gathering all of this information, it will give you an overall picture of the present state of affairs. You then need to ask the question – how do I feel about what I see?

● You might feel *very satisfied* with what you see, and that you are using your skills effectively, your lifestyle fits in with your values and the constraints seem reasonable.

● You might feel *satisfied with some* of what you see. For instance, you are using your skills effectively but your lifestyle does not fit in with your values and some constraints are out of balance.

● Or sadly, you might feel *unsatisfied with all* that you see. You are not using your skills effectively, your lifestyle does not fit with your values and too many constraints are stifling you.

Once again, it would be beneficial to list those areas with which you are satisfied and dissatisfied. This will help you identify changes you want to make for your future and whether or not portfolio working would be compatible with those things you would like to see differently in your future. With this in mind, having made an assessment of the present – where I am now? – it is time to move on the most difficult stage – the future – where am I going?

Where am I going?

This is the million-dollar question, and I certainly do not have the answer for you! The answer will come through exploration and searching for spiritual guidance. This is where we begin the final stage.

This will not be an in-depth study of God's guidance. As I have discovered, however, without beginning here we would be acting totally outside of our faith as Christians. I have made mistakes by trying to take my future into my own hands and I have found blessing in those times when I have sought divine guidance.

'Trust in the Lord with all your heart and lean not on your own understanding; in all your ways acknowledge him, and he will make your paths straight' (Prov. 3: 4-6).

If we do not take this verse to heart, the danger is that we get out guidance from elsewhere, or we struggle along making choices on our own. The challenge is how do we receive God's guidance? Some people would have us believe that there is some 'magic' formula for hearing from God. Some would try to convince us that God uses

gimmicks to speak to us. I have heard stories of people saying that God revealed his will through advertisements, bill-
boards at the side of the road, or by them picking up the
Bible and pointing at random to a verse. Perhaps God does
choose to use these methods. I do believe, however, that
God's guidance goes deeper than the flash of an advert or
a chance verse of Scripture.

Richard Foster, in *Celebration of Discipline*, makes a very
pertinent point when he says 'The specific goal of guidance is not specific instructions about this or that matter
but conformity to the image of Christ… specific guidance
in particular matters is a happy by-product of this goal
having worked its way into our lives… the will of God is
discovered as we become acquainted with God, learn his
ways and become his friend.'[5]

Discovering God's will for our lives goes beyond just
asking the questions: Where should I work? What subjects should I do at university? Should I work for an
employer, or should I set up my own business? As we
grow in intimacy with Christ, we will begin to know
instinctively which of our actions are pleasing to him,
when our decisions are within his will and when we are
being obedient.

There are times, however, when we need to take steps
to try and discover what the will of God is on specific
issues. You may be asking for guidance on such questions as: What is my purpose? What is my primary vocation? What are the roles and activities in which I need
to be involved? Is my ministry in the workplace, community, local church or a combination of these? I have
developed a simple process called PLUTO that can help
you:

Pray and fast to help you focus
Listen to God
Understand yourself – your gifts, passions, values, skills
Talk to others for testing
Open doors to explore options

During this process, you may find it helpful to use imagery once again. Take another blank sheet of paper and, using images, draw a picture of the future you believe God is asking you to create. If you prefer a more structured approach, you may want to write down some general headings. Some people prefer to create a personal mission statement. It doesn't really matter which method you use, as long as you have some indication of the future direction in which the Lord is leading you.

A question I am often asked at this point is `What if I get it wrong?' The truth is that sometimes we may get it wrong, but vocational guidance decisions are rarely irrevocable. Vocational decision-making is not an once-for-all event, but a lifetime process. My own experience is that even when I have got it wrong, God has managed to use my errors to guide me back on the right path. For example, at one stage I had to decide in which area of psychology I was going to specialise. I thought this should probably be cognitive psychology, which would enable me to help marginalised people, so I took a job in a home for people with severe learning disabilities. This was a complete turnaround from all of my experience and education and I eventually realised that this was not the area of psychology that I should be concentrating on. How did I know? Because I never felt at peace with myself or with the work I was doing. I resigned, and began my career in management training, while at the same time doing my Masters degree in occupational behaviour. Although I made the wrong choice initially, God used that opportunity to help me understand what I *should not* be doing which helped me to see what I *should* be doing.

Even if we are fearful that we might take the wrong step, it is important that we take some step rather than no step at all. We need to be reminded of Paul's words in Romans: 'And we know that in all things God works for the good of those who love him, who have been called according to his purpose' (Rom. 8:28). Having sought God's guidance, the challenge is to respond. So the next question is – how am I going to get there?

How do I get there?

Identify each step you will need to take to achieve your vision. Some steps will be immediate or small. Others will be long-term or large. It is helpful to put a time-frame around the steps if possible. So for example you may get a plan that looks like this:

Action	By When
Discuss initial thoughts with spouse/friend/mentor	end of January
Speak to church leaders about contribution to church	end of January
Join community activity	end of January
Investigate training possibilities for learning necessary new skills.	February–March

This is just an example and yours might look quite different. It is important that your plan involves all aspects of life, not just work. You must also recognize that all may not go according to plan, but at least you know the direction you are heading towards. Also, you must continue searching out God's will as his ideas of how to get there will be much better than yours! 'Many are the plans in a man's heart, but it is the Lord's purpose that prevails' (Prov 19:21).

I am not suggesting that this is an easy or simple process, but I cannot emphasise enough how important it is to have some idea of where you are going and how you are going to get there. For some of you, your conclusion will be that you are in the place where you are called to be. Your picture of the future will be more about continuing your calling in a worthy manner. This process will have brought you confirmation, new ideas and renewed vigour or confidence. For others, you may have already had a sense of the direction your life should take and you have already started the journey. This process has just brought affirmation of what you are already doing. Yet for others, this process may have opened up opportunities which you have never seen before. This may bring all kinds of emotions: confusion, excitement, anticipation and possibly even fear. For some, you may be sensing that you are being called to a portfolio lifestyle. If that is the case, then I hope that these next chapters will help you explore the benefits and challenges of living and working in this way.

Whatever the Lord is calling you to do or to be, we can use the words of David and say to the Lord: 'Yet I am always with you; you hold me by my right hand. You guide me with your counsel, and afterward you will take me into glory. Whom have I in heaven but you? And earth has nothing I desire besides you. My flesh and my heart may fail, but God is the strength of my heart and my portion forever' (Ps. 73:23-26).

[1] R. Banks and R. Paul Stevens, *The Complete Book of Everyday Christianity* (Downers Grove, Illinois: InterVarsity Press, 1997), p. 1078

[2] Banks and Stevens, *The Complete Book of Everyday Christianity*, p. 1078

[3] There are many in-depth tools and methods which are too comprehensive to include in this book, including various psychometric and personality-type tests. If you are interested in this type of analysis there is a list of helpful organisations at the end of this book.

[4] John W. Hunt, *Managing People at Work* (England: McGraw-Hill, 1992), pp. 15-33

[5] Foster, Richard, *Celebration of Discipline* (London: Hodder and Stoughton, 1999), p. 236

4

Creating a Portfolio Lifestyle

For those on the threshold of a move into a portfolio lifestyle there are some important questions which need to be addressed. What are the *different types* of portfolio lifestyle? How do we establish *networks* to create our portfolio? How do we *sell* ourselves? How do we *resource* ourselves? How do we manage our *finances*? These are the most frequent questions which I am asked by others considering this type of work. In this chapter I will give some practical suggestions on how to create a portfolio lifestyle.

Types and varieties of portfolio lifestyle

There are many ways of creating a portfolio lifestyle: sometimes it can develop in a reactive manner, responding to requests as and when they arrive. This may work in the short term, but it is more beneficial to clarify the type of portfolio you wish to construct – this leads to better time management and more reliable financial planning. There are a number of different types and approaches to portfolio working, which could be categorised as:

- **Consultancy portfolio:**Increasing numbers of people offer their services as consultants. Such individuals will view themselves as freelance, and will work for a number of organisations at the same time.
- **Part–time combination portfolio:** This will consist of two or three part–time roles, all operating at the same time. These may be a combination of paid and unpaid roles. This provides security of regular income but also releases time for developing opportunities in a range of roles.
- **Compound portfolio:** This may well describe many individuals' career paths over the next few years: a succession of contracted part–time employment which is done at the same time as consultancy or project work. There will be periods of intense focus on one particular role or roles.

In identifying these categories of portfolio working it is important to remember that a flexible approach will be essential. You will need to aim to get the mix of roles right for you, if you are to achieve satisfaction within your portfolio and to work efficiently in each of these roles.

If you have a number of goals which you wish to meet, you need to consider the type of roles you wish to develop, the proportion of time you will allocate to each of these roles and the duration of each role. You may choose to focus on two main roles, for example, working part-time for an existing employer while engaging in further study or independent work. Maybe you have a number of projects which would require several intense periods of concentrated work: for example, two to three months each. Alternatively, you may have a couple of project ideas which would require six months or a year to fulfil, in which case you may wish to explore the possibility of a career break with your employer.

You can easily move between the different varieties of portfolio lifestyle, but there are certain key strategies that you will have to develop. Three of the most crucial strategies for you to consider are networking with other people, resourcing yourself and selling yourself.

Networking

There is an old adage, 'it is not what you know; it is who you know'. We use networks in our social lives to find out about shops, plumbers, restaurants, theatre productions and so on. In fact, many of my opportunities are often a result of an introduction through an established friend, relation or colleague. These contacts even grow without much planning and organisation on my part. However, if you are developing a portfolio of work, you will need to identify who your useful contacts are. And you will also have to consider moving beyond the friendships and social groupings that you already belong to. In developing a range of useful contacts, it is important to bear in mind the following points:

● **You know more people than you realise:** For the purpose of networking you may find that you know more people than you thought. Relations, friends, church members, former work colleagues, neighbours, old friends from school or university, sports partners, service providers – all of these are potential contacts in 'other worlds' outside your existing work context. Often these individuals will be pleased to share their insights and knowledge of their world with an interested individual. Furthermore, these individuals each have their own circle of contacts.

- **It takes longer than you realise:** Some short-term contacts can be developed quickly through existing mutual friendships, but to develop a sustainable extended network will take time. I know of a company director who spent ten years developing friendships and contacts prior to realising any particular benefit for his own portfolio. When he began to approach his network for specific help with establishing his own business, they were only too happy to respond. They had received a great deal from him over a long period of time: now they were happy to repay it. You may, however, need to be prepared to make a long-term investment into the lives of other people before drawing on those friendships.

- **Quantity and quality:** It is important not to bite off more than you can chew when building your network, and occasionally it may be better to turn down the possibility of a new relationship which will take up time that should be devoted to more important contacts. You need to decide which relationships are most important and make sure you give them priority. For example, I have many colleagues with whom I need to spend time in order to maintain my training consultancy work. I have to make a considered decision about what type of training work I want to be doing, and this helps me focus my networking.

- **Enjoy it!** Having suggested the importance of clearly stating the aims of meeting someone, it is important to note that not every conversation we have should be conducted with an agenda in mind. There is a time for honest agenda–driven networking, but there is also a time for getting to know people for the sheer fun of doing so. A stimulating conversation, a refreshing friendship, a good laugh, are all part of the celebration of how God has formed us. Avoid the trap of seeing every interaction as a potential networking or business opportunity. We need to know when we are networking and when we are just socialising. It is helpful to define those times when you are arranging to develop a business relationship which will add potential to your own portfolio and when you are simply enjoying someone else's company.

In considering your own networking, you may find it helpful to take a blank piece of paper and in the middle of the page draw a circle, which will represent you. Then think of all the people who already exist in your network. Write their names around the circle. Then add those whom you don't actually know but who would be good to have in your network. Once you have done this picture, identify which of these relationships would be key to you at this time and plan a strategy for developing your network based on these relationships.

As you begin to arrange meetings with your contacts you will need to consider, 'How am I going to sell myself?'

Selling yourself

A personal marketing strategy will be needed if you are to progress. For some, this will be one of the most difficult parts of developing a portfolio, particularly if you are reserved and uncomfortable with 'blowing your own trumpet'. But it will be necessary if you want to ensure that you get the best opportunities possible.

Application forms, letters and creating your CV are the initial steps in marketing. When developing your CV make sure you identify the skills which you want to use in your portfolio. Give examples of how you have used these in your previous experience. It will also be useful to have recommendation letters from people in your network. For example, you may know someone who works in the same profession or industry as a potential client, and their recommendation will give you more credibility. So if I was trying to get some work with an academic institution, I could ask one of the professors I work with at the London Business School to write me a recommendation. All of my consultancy work has been the result of being recommended by colleagues in my network.

You may need to use formal advertising, structured contacts and agency services as part of your marketing strategy. For example, peripatetic music teachers may wish to use an established agency to make contact with potential pupils. Actors and after-dinner speakers may utilise the services of an agent to develop engagements and to manage and negotiate fees. Freelance musicians may advertise their services in appropriate journals. Business consultants could advertise via professional bodies, such as the Institute of Personnel Development and business schools, as well as in specific professional journals which relate to the various spheres of business such as accountancy, human resources, risk and strategic management.

There are many potential strategies. Everyone developing a portfolio has a unique mix of skills which need to be sold appropriately. With this mind, there are a few general principles that need to be part of every portfolio worker's marketing strategy:

- Close contacts are the best starting point for developing your portfolio but be continually looking out for new possibilities.
- The hardsell may be off-putting to some potential clients, but under-selling yourself can create a loss of confidence in others.
- Not every potential opportunity will come to fruition. Recognise this and be prepared to accept some disappointments.
- Consider how you will close the deal, and don't be afraid to walk away from unfavourable terms. Remember to ask for what you want.
- Have appropriate ideas, documents and contracts prepared for when your services are required.
- Don't neglect your best or long-established clients. Treat them well and don't ignore them when pursuing exciting new projects.
- Don't wait until you've completed your present role to begin developing your next role.

In order to sustain a portfolio you will need to continually sell yourself. If you do not, you can end up at a dead end – without any work roles!

Resourcing yourself

Another important aspect of ensuring employability is *resourcing* yourself: making sure you keep yourself up to date with the skills and knowledge necessary in your chosen profession. In considering how you should resource yourself for your portfolio lifestyle, it is important to recognise the skills you can already offer to clients, colleagues or organisations. These skills and abilities should be further developed both through informal and formal training. Sometimes it can be helpful to obtain formal qualifications to add credibility to your portfolio, though these aren't always necessary.

After working as a consultant for a few years, I realised that having a Masters degree would add to my credibility as well as broaden my perspective on organisational behaviour issues. So at this stage, I did a two-year, part-time MSc in Organisational Behaviour. I was able to do this by distance learning, so I could work it around my domestic and work circumstances.

A few years ago, I felt that my skills as a trainer could be improved. So I took classes with a professional actor on performing techniques. This raised my communication skills as well as giving me confidence in speaking to larger audiences. You may want to shadow another professional or do some work experience in order to develop your skills. Many firms will be pleased to allow you access to a short period of observation or work-shadowing. Such periods of work experience or shadowing could be facilitated through your networks and can also help to widen your network of contacts.

You may need to keep up to date with the latest research through reading journals and magazines, attending conferences, lectures, and watching specialist television programmes.

There are so many ways we can resource ourselves. It is very important if you want to increase your employability, that you continually develop your skills. Lifelong learning is a reality in a world where information and theories develop at such a rapid rate. If you do not sell and resource yourself, you will not be able to provide the finance which you require to live. This leads us to our next question: 'How do I manage the finances?'

Financial issues

I often meet people who love the idea of a portfolio lifestyle, but are put off by the financial risks it seems to involve. Money becomes the main issue which influences their decision to stay in a 'secure' job which provides a regular income. This is understandable in that we all have financial issues to consider: mortgages, pensions, savings, insurance, tax, household bills, the list goes on. It is possible with careful planning to develop a portfolio lifestyle that can provide the necessary financial security. This can only be done by a thorough budgeting process.

Short-term budgeting

Portfolio working does not always provide a regular monthly income, although you will still have regular expenses. You need to start by working these out in order to determine how much you need to earn throughout the year.

When planning your personal and household budget, make a list of all your essential expenditure: monthly bills, food, insurance, utilities, clothing for children, education, and so on. This will give you a bottom-line figure for your outgoings. Having done this, add on an amount for non-essential spending. This will vary for different people, but you need to be very honest and realistic in this area. Your shopping habits are unlikely to change very much. List the amounts you spend on clothes, music, books, magazines, entertainment and gifts.

You may need to consider whether or not you can manage on a reduced level of income. We all have a combination of necessary spending and luxury spending. Try to work out whether you are wasting money on items or activities which don't add much to your overall quality of living. You may even consider downgrading your home or car. When my husband and I first began building our portfolio lifestyles, we bought two older cars. These would not have been our first choice, but we knew that we could not afford to spend a lot on our cars. We had to keep down our overheads as much as possible.

Small businesses will usually plan for unexpected costs. The budget for a project needs to include an amount set aside for 'contingencies'. Your personal budget also needs to include such amounts. So on your list of essential and non-essential expenses, I suggest you add on another 5% for unexpected eventualities.

Long-term budgeting

As well as your unexpected monthly expenses, you also need to consider *longer-term* contingencies. You may need to set aside some *savings* before you move out of your present 'secure' job. It is best to get some advice on the best way to save money. There are many ways of saving and investing money that could provide a financial safety-net for you. We were told when we first started out that we should have at least one year's salary in savings. Of course we did not have this right away, but we worked hard to get this amount saved as soon as we could. An important reason for doing this is that sometimes clients do not pay on time. You will need to be prepared for a lead time, usually 30 days after the invoice date. We have sometimes been fortunate and received payment in two weeks, but have also been in difficulties because we have not been paid for six months. One portfolio worker I know gives a reduction in price for payment within 14 days, but even this does not always encourage prompt payment. So it is best to be realistic about when you will be paid for your services.

It is also important to give consideration to such forms of insurance as mortgage protection schemes, life insurance and disability insurance. These are especially important for the self-employed portfolio worker. You may also want to include private health, education fees and other professional fees in your long-term planning.

Pensions are another serious consideration for the portfolio worker. State pensions and benefits are no longer enough to sustain a reasonable standard of living. Also, in the past, people spent most of their working lives in one company which made company pension schemes the most viable. Now most people move rapidly between organisations and pensions have become more complicated.

You may decide to include a part-time job as part of your portfolio. Often part-time contracts are temporary, but you may be able to discuss the possibility of getting a permanent part-time contract. Decide whether your part-time job makes it worthwhile to opt into a company pension scheme. You may find that it is possible to make additional payments into the company scheme, using money you earn elsewhere. So don't be put off from developing a portfolio lifestyle through fear of not having enough pension later in life. Just as in a traditional job, you will have to plan and take advice.

Tax

You must make sure that you declare all your income to the Inland Revenue. Some of your income might be taxed at source. A company employing you part-time will ensure that tax on that part of your income is taken out before your salary is paid to you. It is vital to take advice on the tax that should be paid on any other income.

The first step will be to register as self-employed. At the end of each tax year you will receive tax forms from the Inland Revenue. These will ask you to state how much you have earned from any sources over the previous year. Make sure that you keep good records of any money that is paid to you. If you are only earning a few thousand pounds a year from self-employed work you may be tempted to 'simplify' arrangements by not keeping proper records.

This could mean that you do not pay enough tax. Eventually, however, the Inland Revenue will find out and you may end up facing a large tax bill with additional penalties. If you don't have good records to refer to, the experience will be even more traumatic.

Ensure that your self-employed work is actually 'self-employment.' If you are working for one company and only getting regular income from that employer then you are not really self-employed. Your employer should provide you with a contract. The company should also be paying the employers' National Insurance contributions.

If your portfolio of roles expands or your income levels rise then self-employment may not be the best route. It may be best to set up a company. This will provide a legal framework which increases your responsibilities but also increases your rights. There might also be significant financial benefits but you will need to take professional advice if you are considering this step.

Make sure that you include saving for tax bills as part of your annual budget! I know too many people who have been caught out, including myself, and not had the money to pay their tax. Estimate which tax bracket you think you will come into and save that percentage per month. If you are in the 25% tax bracket, try and set aside 25% per month for your annual tax bill. You may end up paying less than this amount because of the tax relief you will get on expenses, but it is better to have saved too much than too little.

The good news is that by keeping proper records you may benefit by getting lower tax bills. If you are self-employed there are many expenses which can offset your tax bill. For example, if you are working from home, part of your heating and telephone bill could be included on your tax form as expenses.

Having worked all of these things out, you can decide whether the income from your different roles will enable you to become a portfolio worker. It may be that you have discovered that your monthly spending will be greater than your monthly income (initially). You have two choices – you can either spend less or earn more. Either way, by planning your monthly budget you will be in a position to make decisions about developing a portfolio lifestyle.

Whatever you choose to do – part-time contracts, self-employment, or setting up your own company – pay for the advice of a financial adviser or accountant. The amount of money you will save will be worth their fees. The knowledge that you have sorted out your money will give you security and peace of mind.

Having outlined the practical considerations of finances, I would like to assure you that for most portfolio workers I know, financial ruin has not occurred. Some have had difficult times, but in the end have been able to provide for themselves and their dependants. Portfolio working can seem more risky than a secure and structured approach to work, but if this is the lifestyle you are called to, the benefits outweigh the risks. There will be times when things feel out of control and a bit shaky and you will have to remind yourself that you have a rock on which to stand. 'The Lord is faithful to all his promises and loving towards all he has made' (Ps. 145:13).

5

Managing a Portfolio Lifestyle

Help! My life is out of control. I have too many roles to play, too many people expecting things from me, too many places to be all at once. This will be the cry of many a portfolio worker, as it has been mine more times than I want to admit in my ten years of attempting to manage my portfolio. Managing this type of lifestyle will be both exciting and challenging and will go well beyond the simplistic theories of time management.

There are a number of essential elements which need to be part of your strategy. These include maintaining your equilibrium and your relationships and a persistent evaluation of your focus. Being aware of these challenges in advance will hopefully enable you to avoid some of the pitfalls.

Maintaining equilibrium

Whatever we do in life, it is important that we strive for balance in our spiritual growth, physical and mental health and emotional fulfilment. Because a portfolio requires juggling a number of roles, achieving this equilibrium can be very demanding. It will be important in your planning that you allocate time for exercise, rest, spiritual growth and leisure activity. You will need to aim to achieve a balance between the time you spend on domestic activities, family interaction, local church meetings, paid work, voluntary work and social functions. The appropriate allocation of your time is essential for a successful portfolio.

The question is, 'How do you manage to achieve equilibrium?' The honest answer is that most of the time you will be *striving* to achieve the balance – sometimes you will make it and a lot of the time you won't! It is crucial you take steps towards achieving as much balance as possible, even if you don't manage constant equilibrium. I have a few suggestions which may help you towards this goal.

Say no!

One of the biggest challenges of a portfolio lifestyle is having the courage to say no to projects, requests, new clients, voluntary work, extra church activities and anything else people throw your way. There are a number of reasons why you may find it difficult to do so.

Firstly, there is the risk that if we say no, particularly to paid work, we may never get any more opportunities. There is always that fear of not earning enough money to meet our basic financial needs. That is why it is so important to be very clear about how much money we actually need for survival. This will enable us to say no more often.

Sometimes we may not feel justified in refusing a request for favours either from friends, our local church or perhaps a colleague. A difficulty for a portfolio worker is that to others, it can seem that you have a lot of spare time because you are not always perceived to be working. It is important that you allocate time in your diary very specifically for your different roles as well as time for preparation, domestic, leisure and spiritual activities. That way when you are asked to do favours for others you can be clear as to whether you have the time available. It is much easier to say no when you are in control of your time.

Another reason we may not say no is because we find the new opportunities so exciting we cannot resist the temptation to take them all on. For example, your diary is looking busy, but balanced. Then a publisher approaches you with a request to write a book – a new and exciting project. What do you do – say no or risk overload? Risk overload, of course!!

It is imperative that you learn to say no, and that expectations are managed appropriately.

Clarify expectations

This is fundamental to your attempts to maintain equilibrium. Expectations need to be clear with regards to your paid work, unpaid work and relationships.

Firstly you need to clarify expectations before you start any new project or work. Self-employed consultants should establish appropriate contractual agreements. It is necessary to clarify and discuss what you are able to contribute and to highlight where expectations are unrealistic. The risk for those new to portfolio working, is that a lack of confidence may cause them to yield too much. Peoples' expectations and parameters may not be as high and broad as you imagine them to be. Clarifying expectations at the initial stages of discussion about a project or job will help prevent misunderstandings further down the line.

If you are choosing to devote part of your portfolio to voluntary work the same rule applies. You must be clear about what you can give and clarify what the other parties' expectations are, particularly with regards to time. Often it is our volunteer work that can end up 'stealing' our time because it is not so clear-cut as working for a specified project, a set amount of time and for a fixed payment. Once again, clarification will not only help you maintain a balance but will lessen the possibilities of the relationship being damaged because of mismanaged expectations.

It is also important to clarify the expectations of your family and friends. As I mentioned earlier, there can be the misconception that because you have flexibility this means availability. This is a particular challenge if you are working from home. I have to be very clear with my family of the times when I am available and those when I am not. Just because I am at home does not mean that I am available for domestic purposes. This is not to say we cannot be flexible, but from my own experience I have found that by clarifying expectations it has made it easier for all of us to create the divide between home and work.

Plan your time

One of the keys to establishing balance will be defining how you should be spending your time. You will need to define your priorities on an annual, monthly, weekly and daily basis. These will need to include those elements mentioned before – financial, emotional, spiritual and physical. For example, each year you will need to think about how much you need to earn to cover your expenses, how many weeks holiday you want to take and the other days off you want throughout the year. You will also need to add in time for special occasions, such as family occasions, weddings, your children's exam time, and development days for yourself. Also remember to include retreat times to ensure you do not leave your spiritual growth out of the picture. Once you have put all of these times in your diary, this will show you what you have left. Then you can be in control of what you do with the rest of your available time.

Your priorities will need to be constantly evaluated in the context of changes which occur, such as when work demands increase, the domestic situation requires more attention, or God prompts you to focus on one role in particular. As an example, this year I had two changes which have radically changed the way I planned my year. One was a decision to spend less time with the Mission Team and more time doing consulting work. This was a deliberate decision which I made, based on what my contribution to the team needed to be at this stage and the strong calling I felt back into the workplace. Therefore in planning my work for the year I knew that 50% of my time would be spent consulting rather than the 30% of the last 3 years. Also, every two years I have a 4-5 week commitment teaching leadership skills for the Salvation Army in South America and this was the year for that trip. So in establishing my priorities for this year, both of these had an impact on my planning.

Another example of my context changing was a few years ago when my stepson was taking his GCSEs and my stepdaughter was getting married. I knew that my attention and energy would need to be focused on my home and family and I therefore made the choice to reduce my work considerably – both paid and unpaid. This felt very risky but looking back it was definitely the best choice. I had the time to be available whenever I was needed and I did just enough work to remain in the consultancy network. In fact, by reducing my work level I was able to re-evaluate what type of work I wanted to involved in and ever since that mini-sabbatical, I have made much more focused choices about what work I become involved with.

The way we plan our time is very personal. Your type of work, personality and environments in which you work and live will have an impact on the way you manage your time. For example, if your work responds to the needs of others, such as a consultant who comes in to solve problems, you will need to have a very flexible diary so you can respond when the need arises. On the other hand, some will have work that is very predictable, and combining two part-time roles will make the managing of their diary more straightforward.

Your personality will also have an effect on how you manage your diary. If you are not a detailed person then it is unlikely that a detailed diary system will work for you. If you dislike technology then trying to use a palm-top diary is also unlikely to be a successful strategy. Try different options of diary systems until you find one that suits you. You will know when you have found it because it will become an aid to your survival rather than an irritation.

Allocating time to your important roles first will allow you to fit the other smaller parts of your life in. Stephen Covey, on the video *First Things First*,[1] provides a useful illustration of stones in a bowl. If the large stones are put into a bowl first then a lot of smaller stones can be added later, and so the bowl holds more. Fill the bowl with the small stones first, however, and there will not be room for the larger stones, so the bowl holds less.

Juggling a number of roles and responsibilities can create periods of intense activity. While this can sometimes be stimulating and invigorating, it can also become addictive and eventually lead to exhaustion. You will need to decide what your most important roles are, bearing in mind the need for balance between a variety of life roles, and then plan your time accordingly.

Maintaining relationships

In your attempt to juggle your roles it is crucial that you do not forget to maintain your relationships. Relationships should be one of the higher goals of your portfolio, particularly those with your family, friends and, most importantly, God. Relationship is fundamental to the very nature of our God, as we can see from the Trinity. Jesus is our best example: he considered the relationship with his Father and his people to be his highest priority. A portfolio of preaching, teaching and healing did not crowd out the time for relationships. In fact, it seems that relationships enabled and facilitated his wider ministry.

Family and friends

Busyness can obscure our need for intimacy. Don't make the mistake of allowing portfolio working to crowd out your family relationships and friendships. It is so easy in the excitement of fresh challenges and striving to meet financial needs to neglect the deeper needs for longer-term fulfilment through relationship – with God and others.

Make the effort to plan time with friends, family and your community. Some of my portfolio worker colleagues put these dates in their diaries. This may sound too deliberate and maybe even false, but they say without these times in their diaries, time would run away and they would look back and see that they have not spent enough time with their important relationships. Don't allow yourself to fall into the trap of squeezing out the time you spend with family and friends.

Colleagues

In order to foster good relationships with colleagues you could plan time when you choose to attend the occasional event at which your presence is not strictly necessary. This shows both commitment and also allows 'free time' to develop conversations and friendships. Build in relationship time and get to know your colleagues and co-workers. There is a temptation to see this as wasted time but it should be regarded as invested time. I try to attend at least one lecture a year where I can meet up with my colleagues on a casual basis. I also have a party once a year specifically for business colleagues so we can meet each other's families and just relate to each other socially. Both of these strategies have proved to be very successful in maintaining relationships in an environment where we

operate as a network and sometimes do not work with the
same people for months.

God

If our vocation and lifestyle is to be something which glorifies God then it is necessary to spend time with him. Every
individual, whether following a portfolio lifestyle or not,
encounters threats to the time they spend with God. Those
who are able to maintain a well-ordered and structured diary
will find it easier to establish regular, habitual patterns of
prayer and Bible study. However, for those who do not have
a 9 to 5 job, a structured prayer time may be difficult to sustain and you will therefore need to prepare accordingly.

Your time with God should be at the centre of your
planning and acceptance of roles. If a role is going to
severely disrupt any regular pattern of time with God, then
you should consider the overall impact of that role and
whether it should form part of your portfolio. You will also
need to reflect periodically upon whether you are spending appropriate time following the spiritual disciplines. You
could do this in conversation with a spiritual mentor or
good friend.

Time with God also needs to be considered in the corporate sense. For many portfolio workers allocation of
time with God in the presence of other believers may not
be a priority. If you fail to devote energy to spending time
with God in a corporate context then you are going to
miss out on all the blessings of worshipping with a
Christian community. I try to ensure that at least once a
week I meet with a Christian community, whether that be

on a Sunday or a mid-week meeting. I have found this to be invaluable in supporting a life which does not have any other consistent relationships.

Having mentioned the threats to our time with God, it also important to suggest some of the opportunities which portfolio lifestyle can bring. For some, it is the very desire to develop their time with God that has prompted the move away from a traditional career path. A well-managed portfolio can open up immense opportunities for creating time with God as a central feature of your daily life. You will also have more opportunity, because of the flexibility of your time, for regular periods of retreat or extended reflection. Working from home can be to your advantage because it is possible to allocate some of your best time to prayer and study.

I cannot emphasise enough how important it is to maintain the relationships I have just highlighted. If you do not look after the important friendships in your life, you risk losing them altogether. Also, you will not get the time to re-charge your batteries and release the pressures of juggling your various roles. Without the opportunity for re-charging you could end up at the point of mental and physical exhaustion, with no one to turn to. This may sound extreme, but I know people who have ended up at this point and this is not the place your heavenly Father would want you to be.

Evaluation

Good management of your portfolio will include periodic evaluation of what you are doing and where you are going. Clearing the unwanted stuff from our cupboards is a helpful way of evaluating what we have, deciding what is still useful and getting rid of outdated goods. Likewise with our personal portfolios, a time of evaluating our roles is necessary for us to maintain effectiveness and to ensure that the best job is being done. It is valuable to pause every now and again and ask yourself if you are still going in the right direction, are your activities towards your vision and purpose, are there activities which are no longer necessary to your portfolio?

This is not as easy as it sounds. As we keep things which are no longer useful, or which may even be dangerous, so there is the temptation to hold on to roles which are redundant. Sometimes it is easier to stay on a committee or continue with a project rather than passing it to another person. The reasons for retaining roles are many and varied, but an honest appraisal is necessary if we are not to lose control of our time or lose sight of God's best for our lives.

If you are not good at this yourself, perhaps you could involve a professional and personal mentor to help you. Or maybe you could foster a relationship with another portfolio worker where you discuss plans, prospects, problems and opportunities as well as evaluate your portfolio. I ask for help from the leadership team of the Mission Team who assist me in vetting invitations and my general workload. I also rely on input from my husband and stepchildren who know me well – especially my weakness for taking on too much. All of these people are helpful in challenging me about my attempt to try and do everything!

The result of evaluation may be that you rearrange your portfolio. As I write this book, I am going through a transition of roles myself. As mentioned earlier, I had made a decision to re-allocate the time I am spending in two of my roles. For the last five years I have been strongly involved in the leadership of the Salvation Army Mission Team. This last year has seen a transition in the team with new leadership, which has led me to re-evaluate my involvement. Although the conclusion was emotionally painful, in reality my role in the team is changing from an integral involvement in the team to more of a 'grandparent' role in mentoring and developing the new leaders. This, coupled with a conviction that I should spend more time in the workplace has led me to decrease the time spent with the Mission Team and to increase my consultancy work. Included in this process has been a re-clarification of expectations for all parties involved. Initially I found this to be a very challenging process, but, as time goes on, I am seeing the new leadership team develop and God is opening new doors which I could not have foreseen. This is a good example of the challenging but exciting opportunities which having a portfolio lifestyle can bring.

Celebration

Throughout this book you have been encouraged to consider whether a portfolio lifestyle is God's calling for you and how such a lifestyle is best developed and managed. I want to conclude by suggesting that however you live out your vocation, it should be done as an act of celebration of who God created you to be. Life is not something to be endured or overcome. Although we do experience suffering and pain, in all circumstances we would want to affirm the celebratory nature of our lives.

As participants in God's world we have the opportunity to be part of celebration. Through our lives and how we choose to live our lifestyle, we can add to the creation of the celebration of God. If you could imagine what you would like to achieve, the most fantastic ideas, the greatest roles and goals in your life, what would these look like? Set aside for a moment the processes and principles we have discussed and take this moment to dream, to think big, to let your imagination get carried away. God may envision you for something great, for moving into a place where you leave behind stagnation and dryness and find excitement and purpose. This is part of your participating in the creation of celebration.

A portfolio lifestyle is one way in which a celebration lifestyle can be lived. This is because it can provide opportunities to make choices which can enhance the use of our gifts, talents and creativity. For those living a portfolio lifestyle, it is important to always remember this sense of celebratory purpose. Developing projects, applying for new roles, managing new challenges: all of this is a celebration of the creativity which God has given you.

You have the possibility of developing a lifestyle which is not just about success for 'me' but a lifestyle which can also give something to others through work for charities, church and the community. As Paul said in his farewell to the Ephesians, 'In everything I did, I showed you by this kind of hard work we must help the weak, remembering the words of Lord Jesus himself said; "It is more blessed to give than to receive"' (Acts 20:35). We can celebrate that through the opportunities which we can create to serve others, that we too will be blessed. We can celebrate that we will receive back more than we give, as Jesus told the people during his

Sermon on the Mount: 'Give, and it will be given to you. A good measure, pressed down, shaken together and running over, will be poured into your lap. For with the measure you use, it will be measured to you' (Lk. 6:38).

Also, within our different roles we can be involved in the creation of relationships and the celebration of relationships. Creating relationships at work, at home, in your neighbourhood, and with friends and acquaintances are all expressions of the celebration of God's love. Our portfolio, the mix of context and contact, can be part of a lifestyle which creates relationships that can be channels for God's love. Furthermore, the manifestation of God's love in our relationships is at the core of what it is to be human.

'Why do I do what I do?' is a question that may cross your mind. It is in this context and upon this foundation of living a life of celebration that you can answer it. I encourage you to consider the possibilities of a portfolio lifestyle, within an understanding of life as celebration of the glory of God.

Whatever conclusion you come to, I hope that as a result of reading this book you will be encouraged to take a new step of faith in some area of your life. Even if portfolio working is not your calling, it is my prayer that you will create a lifestyle which celebrates the love God has for you and those around you, a lifestyle which brings you joy and peace as you endeavour to work out those roles to which you are called.

'May the God of hope fill you with all joy and peace as you trust in him, so you may overflow with hope by the power of the Holy Spirit' (Rom. 15:13).

[1] S. Covey, 'First Things First,' from *Time Management to Life Leadership* Video, Covey Leadership Centre Inc, Provo, Utah, USA, 1996

Appendix A

Career Planning Questionnaire: Skills

Read through the skills under the headings below and give yourself a mark for each one. Use a range of 1 to 6, awarding 6 for a definite skill, 1 for a complete lack of this skill. Then add up your scores for each skill area, so you see where you are strongest. Add any skills you think have been omitted.

Skills	Score
Creative	
Drawing, Painting	....
Design	....
Musical Performance	....
Imagination	....
Creative Writing	....
Other	....
Influencing	
Persuading/Negotiating	....
Selling a Product/Service	....
Managing Other People	....
Organising Events/Activities	....

Promoting Ideas Effectively ....
Other ....

Communicating

Using the Written Word ....
Translating Foreign Languages ....
Reporting on Events ....
Speaking in Public ....
Understanding Written Material ....
Other ....

Problem solving

Analysing Information ....
Using Maps or Diagrams ....
Servicing Equipment ....
Following Detailed Instructions ....
Assembling Parts/Components ....
Other ....

Social

Relating to a Wide Range of People ....
Giving Help/Support to Others ....
Showing Insight/Understanding ....
Teaching/Training ....
Building Relationships ....
Other ....

Numerical

Interpreting Graphs/Statistics	....
Handling/Manipulating Data	....
Using Computers	....
Solving Quantitative Problems	....
Producing Accounts/Budgets	....
Other	....

Physical

Using Hand/Power Tools	....
Operating Machinery	....
Manual Dexterity	....
Physical Stamina	....
Tending Plants/Animals	....
Other	....

Skill area score — Total Score

Skill area score	Total Score
Creative	....
Influencing	....
Communicating	....
Problem solving	....
Social	....
Physical	....
Numerical	....

Appendix B

Work Values Questionnaire

(1 = strongly disagree; 10 = strongly agree)

I would prefer a job where:	Score
I can get ahead with my career (A)	....
I can help people cope better with their lives (Sv)	....
There is high financial reward (E)	....
Job security is guaranteed (Se)	....
I can work independently of others (I)	....
I can do things which involve some risk (R)	....
I can enjoy high social status (P)	....
There is quite a bit of travel (V)	....
I can enjoy my place of work (En)	....
I can do work that is socially useful (Sv)	....
I can develop new ideas of products (C)	....
There is little work-related stress (Se)	....
People respect me for my position (P)	....
There is plenty of scope for advancement (A)	....
There are new challenges and ventures (R)	....
Things are left entirely to my own judgement (I)	....
There is a pleasant working environment (En)	....
I am in charge of other people (Au)	....

I can work as part of a team (S) ....

I can be creative or inventive (C) ....

A very good standard of living is possible (E) ....

There are friendly people around me (S) ....

There is a lot of variety in what I do (V) ....

I have the authority to get things done (Au) ....

Now add up the scores according to the code alongside each item and fill in the score sheet below. You will find that every statement falls into one of 12 value categories. The score itself is not important: what matters is which values you rank higher than others.

SCORE SHEET

Value	Score
Advancement (A)	
Upward mobility and promotion; more interesting work	....
Social (S)	
Friendly contact with colleagues	....
Attending to and talking to people	....
Economic (E)	
High salary and financial rewards	....
Security (Se)	
Job stability and regular income	....
Well-being not threatened	....

Independence (I)
Autonomy: freedom to make decisions and
take the initiative ....

Prestige (P)
Being seen in an important role ....
Social, economic or occupational status ....

Variety (V)
Change and variety in tasks and place of work ....

Environment (En)
Pleasant physical surroundings ....

Serving (Sv)
Helping people; work of social or community
value ....

Creative (C)
Being original: creating new products ....
Finding different solutions ....

Risk (R)
An element of uncertainty ....
Financial and other kinds of risk ....

Authority (Au)
Influence and control over people ....
Leading others and making decisions ....

Useful Organisations

Career Counselling Services
46 Ferry Rd
London
SW13 9PW

Careers And Occupational Information
Centre (COIC)
St Mary's House
Moorfoot
Sheffield
S1 4PQ

Career Research & Advisory Centre
(CRAC)
Sheraton House
Castle Park
Cambridge
CB3 0AX

Counselling And Career Development
Unit (CCDU)
University Of Leeds
44 Clarendon Rd
Leeds
LS2 9PJ

Useful Organisations

Institute Of Careers Guidance (ICG)
27a Lower High St
Stourbridge
West Midlands
DY8 1TA
www.icg-uk.org

National Institute Of Career Education And
Counselling (NICEC)
Sheraton House
Castle Park
Cambridge
CB3 0AX